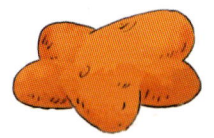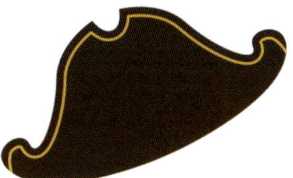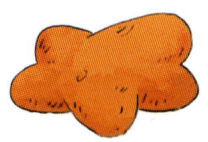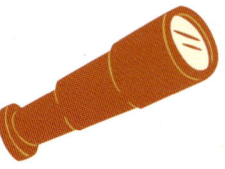

To Aidan,
when you dream,
anything is possible.
XOXO KA

Where Do Pirates Go On Vacation?

Published by Lucky Four Press, LLC, 2022
Copyright ©2022 Kim Ann / Lucky Four Press, LLC
Library of Congress Number: 2022920371

Printed in the USA and China. All rights reserved.
No part of this book may be reproduced in any form
without the written permission of the copyright holder.

Inquiries should be directed to: info@authorkimann.com.
www.authorkimann.com

ISBN-13: 978-1-953774-43-9 Paperback
ISBN-13: 978-1-953774-44-6 Hardcover

Where Do Pirates Go on Vacation?

by Kim Ann

Illustrated by Nejla Shojaie

2023

To: Charlotte ♡
Look for treasure around every corner!
xoxo ♡
Kim Ann

Where do pirates go when there's no treasure to be found?

Do pirates go to a secret island hideaway?

High up in the crow's nests with a spyglass, night and day?

Do pirates go on adventures with their pirate friends?

Shooting down the rapids as the river flows and bends!

Do pirates like fishing, and do they like sailboats too?

Do they travel on yachts when they leave their ships and crew?

Or would they rather just play games when they have a chance?

Gazing up at the stars and the moon's magical light?

Do pirates go on vacations?
Do they get away?

Or are they happy on their ships
each and every day?

Pirates have such exciting lives.
It is crystal clear.

Quick Affirmations Series

Kim Ann
authorkimann.com

 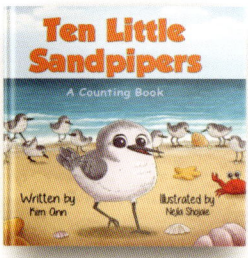 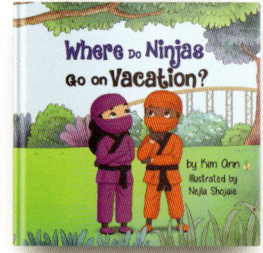 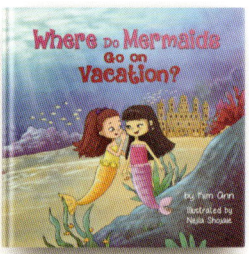

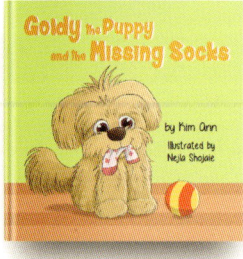 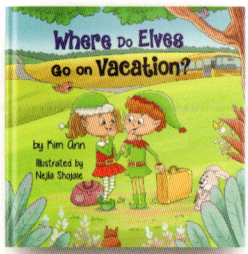 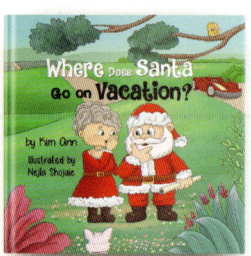 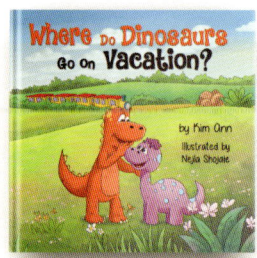 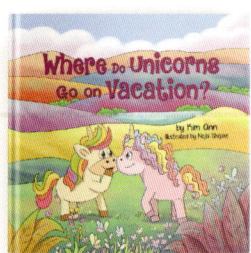

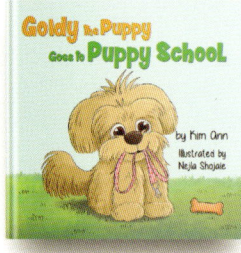  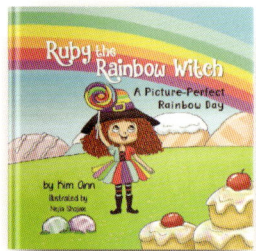 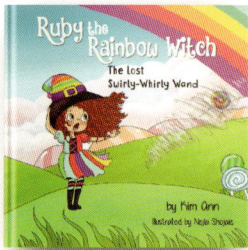 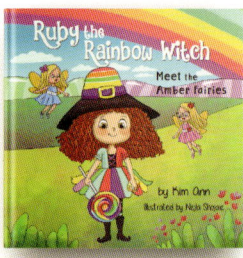

ruby, la brujita arcoiris

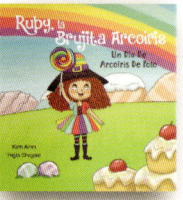 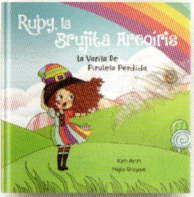 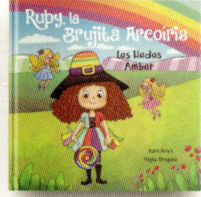

Coloring Books

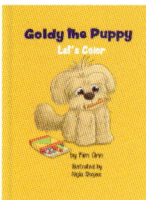 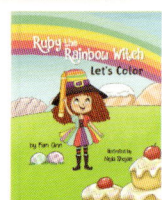

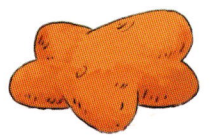

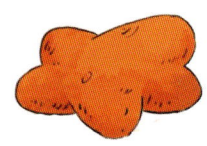

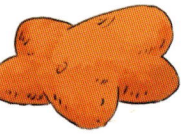